Original title:

Marriage Mechanics

Copyright © 2024 Swan Charm

Author: Mirell Mesipuu
ISBN HARDBACK: 978-9916-89-214-5
ISBN PAPERBACK: 978-9916-89-215-2
ISBN EBOOK: 978-9916-89-216-9

The Art of Union

When hearts align, a bond is formed,
In silken threads, love is warmed.
Each moment shared, a treasure dear,
In whispers soft, our path is clear.

Cities fade, yet we remain,
Together dancing through the rain.
With every challenge, side by side,
In the art of union, we confide.

Bridging Hearts

Across the miles, we find a way,
With every word, the shadows sway.
From silence grows a vibrant song,
In this connection, we belong.

Hearts like rivers, flowing free,
Merging gently, you and me.
Building bridges with our dreams,
In a world that softly gleams.

Woven Promises

Threads of hope in tapestry,
With every stitch, our legacy.
Promises made with earnest care,
In every moment, we declare.

Through trials faced, we stand as one,
With woven hearts, our spirits run.
In every pattern, love appears,
A fabric rich, with joy and tears.

The Framework of Us

In the framework built of trust,
Support and love, a must.
Each beam a memory we've made,
In the sunlight, shadows fade.

Every heartbeat, a solid plank,
In unity, we take our rank.
Together sturdy, come what may,
In the framework, we'll always stay.

The Fabric of Forever

Threads of time weave our tale,
Stitching moments, soft yet frail.
In love's loom, we find our grace,
Each heartbeat, a warm embrace.

Patterns shift, yet hearts stay true,
A tapestry, me and you.
Colors fade but never part,
Forever woven, heart to heart.

The Unseen Bond

In silence speaks a gentle thread,
An energy that's softly spread.
Through eyes that hold a secret light,
We dance in shadows, day and night.

A bond unspoken, yet so near,
In every laugh and whispered cheer.
Though words may fail, our souls align,
Together, we are truly fine.

Charting New Paths

Under stars, we make our way,
With courage bold, we won't delay.
Each step we take, a choice we claim,
Exploring wild, igniting flame.

Through thick and thin, hand in hand,
We craft our dreams upon this land.
New horizons call our name,
In every heartbeat, sparks of flame.

A Balancing Act

On a tightrope, we find our stance,
In the whirlwind of this dance.
Life's ups and downs, we navigate,
With hope and love, we levitate.

One step forward, then a sway,
Finding strength in the fray.
Balance found in trust and grace,
Together we embrace this space.

The Fusion of Two

In the dance of light and shade,
Two hearts beat, unafraid.
With every glance, a spark ignites,
Drawing close on starry nights.

Whispers soft, like gentle streams,
Woven tight in shared dreams.
Hand in hand, we brave the tide,
Together, we shall abide.

Through storms that howl and winds that moan,
Together, we have grown.
In the warmth of love's embrace,
We find our sacred space.

With every challenge, we unite,
Turning darkness into light.
In this journey, side by side,
Two souls as one, our hearts collide.

In the tapestry of time,
Our love's rhythm is a rhyme.
As every moment we renew,
Together, we are the fusion of two.

Cascading Circles

In ripples soft, circles arise,
Beneath the vast, open skies.
Each wave a story to be told,
In colors bright, and shadows bold.

As they swell and gently blend,
Life's secrets begin to mend.
The pulse of nature sings its song,
In circles wide, where all belong.

From one to many, spirals grow,
In harmony, their power flows.
Connected by an unseen thread,
New beginnings, fear shed.

In each circle, laughter rings,
Unity in small, simple things.
As gentle sighs and joyful turns,
The flame of love within us burns.

Forever flowing, never still,
Cascading circles, hearts to fill.
In every twist and every bend,
The dance of life shall never end.

Connected in Parallel

Two lives charted side by side,
In paths where hidden dreams abide.
With silent strength, we walk aloof,
Bound by fate, in love's own proof.

Through tangled woods and winding ways,
Our spirits bright, in golden rays.
Connected deep, though miles apart,
Each step echoes in the heart.

In quiet moments, thoughts converge,
In cherished memories, we surge.
Through time, in parallel we stand,
Each life a strand by fate's own hand.

The stars above weave tales anew,
In whispers soft, they guide us through.
In every heartbeat, every sigh,
Together still, you and I.

Though roads may twist and shift their course,
Our bond remains a steady force.
In every challenge, near or far,
We shine as one, a guiding star.

The Tapestry of Us

In threads of gold and hues so bright,
We weave our dreams each day and night.
With love as our enduring base,
A masterpiece of time and space.

Every stitch a memory made,
In laughter's joy, in tears displayed.
Through every shade and every hue,
The tapestry tells of me and you.

In silken strands, our stories blend,
A woven tale with no end.
With hands entwined, we work in sync,
Creating magic with every link.

Through storms and sunshine, we embark,
Finding light within the dark.
As life unfolds, forever trust,
The beauty lies in the tapestry of us.

In every fold and gentle seam,
We find the threads of love's own dream.
Together we colors anew,
In the rich tapestry of us, so true.

The Road of Unity

Together we walk, hand in hand,
Through valleys deep, across vast land.
With every step, our spirits soar,
In harmony, we find the core.

Paths may diverge, yet we align,
In laughter and tears, our hearts entwine.
The road is long, but hope remains,
In every joy, in every pain.

The sun will rise, the night will fade,
In this great journey, love won't trade.
Through mountains high and rivers wide,
Unity, our steadfast guide.

Voices merge in a choir's grace,
A tapestry woven in time and space.
Each story shared, a thread we weave,
In this great journey, we believe.

When storms may come to shake our way,
Together we'll stand, come what may.
The road is ours, the path is clear,
In unity, we persevere.

The Joint Venture

In this venture, we stake our claim,
Two hearts entwined, a shared flame.
With visions bold, we chart the course,
Together we rise, a mighty force.

Each dream we chase, a step we take,
In this dance of trust, no hearts will break.
Hand in hand, we'll overcome,
In collaboration, we are one.

Through winding paths, we'll find our way,
With open minds, come what may.
Challenges faced, we'll break the mold,
This joint venture, a tale of gold.

Ideas ignite like stars at night,
In synergy, we'll find the light.
With passion fierce, our dreams unfold,
In this partnership, our hearts are bold.

As tides may turn, and storms may brew,
Together we'll stand, our bond is true.
This journey shared, forever ours,
In unity, we build the stars.

Coalescing Rhythms

In the beat of hearts, we find our song,
Together we dance, where we belong.
With every pulse, the world aligns,
Coalescing rhythms, love entwines.

A melody born from laughter and tears,
In harmony, we silence our fears.
Each note a promise, a gentle sway,
In this symphony, we find our way.

Through trials faced and moments shared,
With every step, we show we cared.
A cadence strong, we lift our voice,
In this connection, we rejoice.

The echoes fade, yet memories stay,
In the quiet moments, love will play.
The rhythm flows, a timeless dance,
In every heartbeat, there's a chance.

With hands held firm, we create the sound,
In each coalescing beat, we're found.
A journey vast, together we roam,
In these rhythms, we find our home.

The Intersection of Hearts

At the crossroads where our paths meet,
Two souls converge, a bond so sweet.
In this moment, the world feels right,
The intersection of hearts, pure light.

With every glance, a story unfolds,
In whispered dreams, our future holds.
In shared laughter, in quiet grace,
We find our truth in this sacred space.

Diverse journeys, yet here we stand,
This union forged, a steady hand.
With every pulse, our spirits blend,
In this crossing, we transcend.

Through winds that shift and trials endure,
In unity's embrace, we are secure.
Each heartbeat echoes, love's refrain,
At this intersection, we remain.

In life's vast tapestry, we are thread,
Woven together, we're softly led.
With every heartbeat, we cultivate,
The intersection of hearts, our fate.

The Weave of Togetherness

In threads of silver and gold,
We gather stories untold.
Each strand a memory bright,
Stitched with laughter and light.

Hands clasped in gentle embrace,
Together, we find our place.
Fingers intertwined, we grow,
In the warmth of love's glow.

Though storms may come our way,
We stand strong, come what may.
A fabric rich and profound,
Where kinship and hope abound.

With every twist and turn,
A lesson keenly learned.
In unity, we rise high,
Underneath the vast sky.

As time weaves its ancient art,
Each bond a beating heart.
Together we face the test,
In this weave, we are blessed.

Piecing Together Forever

A puzzle laid across the floor,
Each piece holds an open door.
With colors bright, we arrange,
Moments sweet, a perfect change.

Fragmented dreams start to blend,
As hearts learn to never end.
Shapes of joy, fragments of tears,
Crafting tales across the years.

Hands eager to fit the part,
Bringing life to every heart.
With patience, we carefully find,
The patterns that love designed.

In shadows of doubt we stand,
Together, we join hand in hand.
With each layer, trust grows near,
Binding us, as we persevere.

Through laughter and through strife,
We piece together our life.
With every win and loss,
In unity, we find our gloss.

The Tapestry of Ties

Woven threads of joy and pain,
In every stitch, there remains.
A tapestry rich and bright,
Reflecting love's pure light.

Each color a different voice,
In this weave, we rejoice.
Bound by dreams and shared fears,
We gather strength through the years.

Patterns formed in trials faced,
With threads of courage laced.
In each corner, hope finds space,
With love, we leave a trace.

Every fray tells a tale,
Of times when we seemed frail.
Yet together we are strong,
In our hearts, we belong.

So let this fabric unfurl,
A profound gift to the world.
In every heart, the ties run deep,
As we dream and never sleep.

The Fusion of Fates

Two paths converge, a single way,
Guided by the light of day.
In every step, a rhythm beat,
Together we feel complete.

The stars above align so bright,
As destinies intertwine at night.
With every breath, we share a space,
In the dance of our embrace.

A journey marked with trust and grace,
Together we find our place.
In silence, whispers softly blend,
As we know, love has no end.

Every tear and every laugh,
Colors weaving our own path.
Through trials fierce, we elevate,
In the fusion we create.

As rivers flow into the sea,
Our lives link, eternally.
In this bond, we find our fates,
A love that never hesitates.

The Machinery of Affection

In gears that laugh, we turn and spin,
Crafting bonds where love begins.
With every tick, a heartbeat's tune,
In the dance, we find our bloom.

Wheels of trust in motion flow,
Oil of kindness helps us grow.
Each part a piece of who we are,
Guided by a brightening star.

Screws that hold our dreams so tight,
Shadows fade in shared daylight.
An engine fueled by gentle grace,
In this machine, we find our place.

Lubricated with whispered sighs,
Together we can touch the skies.
Underneath the iron frame,
Lies a love that knows no shame.

Let's tend the parts, let's keep it strong,
With every day, we right the wrong.
For in this craft, we will invest,
The machinery of love, our quest.

Anchored Together

In the seas where waves collide,
We find strength, with hearts as guides.
Anchored deep in love's embrace,
Together we can face the race.

With sturdy ropes that bind our fate,
We weather storms, we do not wait.
Side by side through ebb and flow,
In every tide, our trust will grow.

The horizon calls, we sail as one,
Under the shade of the blazing sun.
With every whisper of the breeze,
Our laughter carries, hearts at ease.

In twilight's glow, we drop the line,
Finding peace, your hand in mine.
Through trials and triumphs, we remain,
Anchored together, joy or pain.

With every anchor set in place,
We build a haven, a sacred space.
For in this journey, bold and bright,
Together we will find our light.

The Fabric of Fidelity

Woven threads of trust and care,
In every stitch, a promise shared.
Patterns bloom in vibrant hue,
This cloth, our love, forever true.

With needle hearts that sew the seams,
We craft a life from shared dreams.
Each color tells a story sweet,
In this fabric, no deceit.

With every fold, we learn to bend,
Through life's design, we comprehend.
Tangles may arise in time,
Yet our bond remains sublime.

The fabric stretches, strong yet fine,
A tapestry, your hand in mine.
Each woven piece, a memory bright,
Guided softly by love's light.

And as we wrap in warmth's embrace,
We find our strength in love's own grace.
Together, stitched in harmony,
The fabric of fidelity.

The Intricate Weave

In threads of gold and crimson hue,
We weave a tale that feels so true.
Each loop and knot, a memory held,
A tapestry of love, compelled.

With fingers deft, we craft the design,
Two souls entwined, your heart in mine.
Every color a different year,
In this fabric, joy and fear.

Patterns shift as seasons change,
Yet in our weave, we grow, arrange.
Frayed edges tell of battles won,
Strengthened threads in morning sun.

In quiet moments, we stitch anew,
With love's own hand, we'll see it through.
A patchwork quilt of laughter bright,
Together, we are pure delight.

This intricate weave, a work of art,
Crafted gently, piece by part.
Forever bound in each embrace,
In love's embrace, we find our place.

Rivets of Resilience

In storms we stand together,
With strength that never bends,
Our hearts like forged steel,
Forging paths, we make amends.

Through trials and the fight,
We rise, we push, we strive,
Each scar tells our story,
Together, we survive.

With every challenge faced,
Our bonds become so bold,
Like rivets in the frame,
Our tale of hope retold.

The weight we bear as one,
Can't break our unity,
In every fall we rise,
We are our remedy.

In laughter and in tears,
We build from what we've lost,
Resilience is our name,
Together, we pay the cost.

The Piston of Partnership

Two hearts that beat as one,
In tandem, we create,
A rhythm strong and true,
Our future sealed by fate.

In every turn and twist,
We lift each other's weight,
With every pulse we share,
Our bond will navigate.

Each challenge makes us grind,
Yet sparks ignite our drive,
Through friction, we find strength,
In unity, we thrive.

Together, we press on,
Through valleys deep and wide,
The engine of our dreams,
With trust as our guide.

In every push and pull,
We build our solid ground,
Through highs and lows alike,
In partnership, we're bound.

Treads of Trust

On roads we travel far,
With each step, we align,
The paths may shift and change,
But trust will always shine.

Through gravel and through grime,
We conquer every stall,
With treads worn by our journey,
We'll answer every call.

Together we embark,
In shadows and in light,
With every stride we take,
Our hearts are bound so tight.

As seasons come and go,
Our footprints leave a trace,
With trust as our safeguard,
We'll always find our place.

In moments brief and rare,
When doubts may cloud our mind,
We'll tread the path of hope,
With faith, our lives entwined.

A Frame of Forever

In frames built from our dreams,
We sketch our life profound,
With every corner turned,
Together, we are bound.

The walls that hold our love,
Stand strong against the storm,
In memories we create,
Our shelter keeps us warm.

Through ages may we grow,
Our bond won't fade away,
In stitches we will weave,
A tapestry of day.

With every glance we share,
In silence, voices blend,
Within this frame so dear,
We find the strength to mend.

As time may paint us gray,
Our hearts will stay aligned,
In this frame of forever,
True love is always kind.

Converging Journeys

Two paths diverge beneath the trees,
Each whispering tales of flowing breeze.
Two souls walk on, with hearts aligned,
In every step, their fates entwined.

With laughter shared and secrets told,
They venture forth, both brave and bold.
The road ahead, though winding still,
Together strong, they climb the hill.

The sun will set, yet stars will gleam,
Guiding them onward, through life's stream.
Each twist and turn, a chance to grow,
In unity, their courage flows.

Through valleys deep and mountains high,
They seek the dreams that touch the sky.
For every journey must converge,
In love and trust, they find the urge.

And as the days blend into night,
Their spirits dance in soft twilight.
The journey shared, a precious art,
A story penned by every heart.

The Pulse of Partnership

Two hearts beat in a gentle rhyme,
A melody forged through space and time.
In harmony, they find their way,
As dreams converge at break of day.

Through vibrant laughter and silent tears,
They bridge the gap of distant years.
In every challenge, side by side,
Together, they choose love as their guide.

A tapestry woven with threads of grace,
Every moment, they leave a trace.
Through storms and sunshine, hand in hand,
In every heartbeat, they understand.

With trust as roots, their bond will bloom,
In every shadow, they shun the gloom.
For every pass, a rhythm shared,
In partnership, their hearts bared.

As seasons change, they flourish bright,
Navigating life, through day and night.
In the pulse of love, they find their song,
Together forever, where they belong.

The Dance of Duality

Two souls entwined in cosmic sway,
In every motion, night and day.
A balance struck, in perfect grace,
With every step, they find their place.

In joy and sorrow, hand in hand,
They navigate the shifting sand.
A dance of light and shadows cast,
United strong, they hold steadfast.

Through every challenge, ebb and flow,
In moments sweet, together grow.
The beauty lies in contrast bright,
A tapestry of darkness and light.

With laughter echoing through the years,
And whispered dreams that calm their fears.
In every heartbeat, rhythm found,
The dance of duality profound.

As stars align in cosmic play,
They weave their dreams, come what may.
In every twirl, a story told,
A dance of life, both brave and bold.

The Intersection of Dreams

In the quiet dusk where wishes meet,
Two dreams converge, an intricate feat.
A place where hopes and visions blend,
In sacred space, where hearts commend.

Each thought a star that lights the way,
Guiding lost souls through the gray.
At this crossroad, paths intertwine,
Together they spark, a rare design.

With whispered hopes in twilight's glow,
They find the strength to let dreams flow.
In every promise that they share,
Each breath a pledge, a sacred prayer.

Through winding roads and distant lands,
They build a world with loving hands.
At each intersection, they stand tall,
A testament that love can conquer all.

And when the dawn begins to rise,
Their dreams will soar across the skies.
In the beauty of this life, they gleam,
Together forever, in the stream.

Love's Blueprint

In shadows soft, our hearts align,
With gentle hands, we weave the design.
Each thread a promise, pure and true,
In the tapestry of me and you.

Blueprints drawn in stars above,
Mapping out the dance of love.
Mistakes erased, yet hope displays,
A craft refined through endless days.

Moments shared, like whispered dreams,
In every corner, laughter beams.
Within the lines, our stories flow,
Creating paths where feelings grow.

Together, building, brick by brick,
A fortress strong, where hearts can pick.
Through storms and trials, we'll survive,
Our love's true blueprint keeps us alive.

The Architecture of Affection

In every curve, affection glows,
Like arches high, where sunlight flows.
We sketch our wishes upon the page,
Blueprints drawn with love, a stage.

Foundations built on trust and care,
In whispered moments, we both share.
The structure stands, a testament,
That love, like art, is Heaven-sent.

Windows wide, let in the light,
Each beam a promise, bold and bright.
With every nail and careful plan,
We rise together, hand in hand.

Rooms filled with warmth, inviting grace,
In this sweet home, we find our place.
The architecture of our embrace,
Creates a world that time can't replace.

Bolts of Unity

Strong and steady, love's embrace,
Bolts of unity hold our space.
Through trials faced, we stand as one,
In every darkness, we find the sun.

Bound by dreams and hopes we share,
Like iron links, beyond compare.
Fastened tight in each other's hold,
Through whispered tales and the brave and bold.

With every challenge, we will rise,
Forged together, boundless skies.
A strength that comes from shared delight,
In bolts of unity, we ignite.

Through storms that test and winds that blow,
Our hearts as anchors, steady and slow.
In love, we find our truest guide,
In bolts of unity, we abide.

A Symphony of Engagements

In every note, love's music plays,
A symphony that fills our days.
Together we compose a tune,
That dances lightly with the moon.

Strings of laughter, winds of grace,
Echo softly in our space.
We play in harmony, side by side,
In this orchestra, there's no divide.

The rhythm flows, a gentle sway,
As heartbeats join in sweet ballet.
With every chord, our souls entwine,
Creating songs that feel divine.

From soft caresses, crescendos rise,
In tangled arms, love never lies.
A symphony woven through the years,
With melodies born from joys and tears.

An Engine for Love

In twilight's glow, our hearts ignite,
An engine roaring, emotions take flight.
With whispered dreams and gentle grace,
We build our world, a sacred space.

Each glance a spark, each touch a thrill,
Together we soar, over every hill.
Through stormy skies, our love will steer,
In every heartbeat, you are near.

With laughter shared and burdens light,
We find our peace in the quiet night.
The wheels turn round, the rhythm strong,
In the journey of love, forever we belong.

The road ahead, a winding thread,
In passion's fire, we are both fed.
Through trials faced, we still stay true,
An engine for love, just me and you.

As seasons change and time moves on,
In the melody of us, love's song.
With every mile, every passing stare,
In the depths of our souls, our hearts lay bare.

The Cycle of Us

In a dance of time, we find our place,
The cycle of us, a warm embrace.
With every turn, a new dawn breaks,
In the tapestry of love, our hearts awake.

Seasons shift, yet we remain,
Through joy and laughter, through sorrow and pain.
In the ebb and flow, we find our way,
The cycle of us, come what may.

Like the moon and sun, we rise and fall,
In harmony's rhythm, we hear the call.
Through storms we weather, through calm we glide,
In the cycle of us, love won't hide.

Past and future, all intertwined,
In every heartbeat, our souls aligned.
With every breath, new memories we trust,
In the endless dance, the cycle of us.

From the roots we nurture, to the sky we aim,
In every chapter, love's sweet frame.
Through time's embrace, we forever rise,
In the cycle of us, our spirits fly.

Threads of Destiny

In the loom of life, our fates entwine,
Threads of destiny, yours and mine.
With colors bright, we weave and spin,
Together we rise, together we begin.

Each strand a story, each knot a sign,
In the fabric of dreams, our hearts align.
Through trials faced, our bond grows strong,
In the tapestry of time, where we belong.

With every twist, a choice refined,
In the dance of fate, love is defined.
Through the highs and lows, we find our way,
Threads of destiny, come what may.

In quiet moments, we pause and see,
The beauty in the flaws, the harmony.
With open hearts, we face the new,
In the threads of destiny, just me and you.

So let us weave with every breath,
In the artistry of life, defying death.
For in each moment, a chance we trust,
In the threads of destiny, our love is a must.

Composed Harmony

In the stillness, a melody plays,
Composed harmony in countless ways.
With gentle notes that linger on,
A symphony of hearts, in the dawn.

With every heartbeat, we find the song,
In rhythms shared, where we belong.
The echoes dance, in twilight's glow,
In composed harmony, love will flow.

Through laughter and tears, we create the tune,
In the whispers of stars and the light of the moon.
Together we rise, on this journey bright,
In composed harmony, our spirits take flight.

With every challenge, we find the key,
Unlocking the notes of you and me.
As seasons change, our music thrives,
In the beauty of love, our joy survives.

So let us play, our hearts in sync,
In the canvas of time, we beautifully link.
With every sigh, every laugh, every plea,
In composed harmony, just you and me.

Crafting a Lifetime

In whispers of dreams we weave,
Hopes stitched with delicate thread.
Moments thread through time's fabric,
Memories linger, gently spread.

Each choice a brush on our canvas,
Colors blend where futures meet.
With every turn, a story unfolds,
Life's tapestry beneath our feet.

Through laughter and tears, we gather,
Lessons learned in sun and rain.
Each chapter builds our legacy,
Crafting joy from heart's refrain.

As seasons change, so do we,
Renewed with every dawn's light.
In the gallery of our being,
Every heartbeat fuels the fight.

Together we carve a journey,
With every step, a soul's embrace.
In the art of crafting a lifetime,
Love remains our saving grace.

The Engine of Endurance

In the heart where passion ignites,
A fire stirs with fierce desire.
Through trials faced and battles fought,
A spirit forged in endless mire.

Each setback pushes us to rise,
A testament to strength within.
With grit and grace, we tread the path,
The engine roaring, we begin.

In whispers of doubt, we gather,
Fueling dreams with hope anew.
Each stride we take, a promise made,
Resilience shines in all we do.

The road is long, but we press on,
Bound by purpose, true and clear.
For every step brought forth in faith,
Leads us closer, far and near.

Together we are unyielding,
In the storm, we find our way.
The engine of endurance roars,
As courage lights the darkest day.

Aligning Aspirations

In the quiet of a hopeful mind,
Dreams dance like stars in the night.
With purpose guiding every thought,
We chart our course, hearts taking flight.

Each vision crystallizes bright,
A compass to our wildest dreams.
Through valleys deep and mountains high,
We navigate through winding streams.

With every goal, a spark ignites,
Aligning paths with the divine.
As we reach for what we seek,
Our aspirations intertwine.

Together we rise in unity,
With hands clasped, no fear to share.
In the beauty of collaboration,
Our dreams become the answer to prayer.

In the dance of life, we flourish,
Embracing change, we grow anew.
Aligning aspirations in our hearts,
A journey rich with vibrant hue.

Mosaic of Moments

Each moment a tile in our lives,
Laid carefully with love and care.
In colors bright and shades of gray,
A mosaic crafted, beautifully rare.

From laughter shared to sorrows deep,
Every piece tells a story true.
In fragments bright, our lives emerge,
A picture formed from me and you.

We gather memories, rich and vast,
An artful blend of joy and pain.
In this collection, we find our way,
A labyrinth of sunshine and rain.

In the chaos, we find our peace,
Within life's intricate design.
A tapestry of fleeting time,
Each moment a star that brightly shines.

As the seasons change and shift,
We cherish each piece as it comes.
In the mosaic of life's embrace,
We find our rhythm, hearts aligned.

Balancing Acts

In the air we sway and bend,
A dance of grace, we shall not end.
With every step, we find our place,
In harmony, we embrace the space.

With weights of joy and loads of fears,
We balance life throughout the years.
Each moment counts, a careful choice,
In whispered dreams, we find our voice.

The scale may tip, the load may shift,
Yet through it all, we find our gift.
Together here, we stand so tall,
In shared pursuits, we never fall.

With open hearts, we take the leap,
And in the plunge, our secrets keep.
A tether strong, we hold it tight,
In balancing acts, we find our light.

Joined Journeys

Two paths converge beneath the sun,
In step with dreams, two hearts are one.
Through winding trails, we find our way,
In every dawn, a brand-new day.

With laughter shared, we chase the light,
In shadowed corners, hold on tight.
Each twist and turn, a dance of fate,
In every moment, we celebrate.

The road may rise, the road may fall,
Yet side by side, we conquer all.
In whispered hopes, we chart the stars,
Together, beyond our lives' memoirs.

Through storms that howl and nights that chill,
Our love, a fire, a constant thrill.
With hands entwined, we greet the dawn,
In joined journeys, we carry on.

The Design of Together

In threads of gold, our stories weave,
Each stitch a moment we believe.
With patterns bright, in colors bold,
The tapestry of love unfolds.

A canvas stretched, with care and grace,
In every line, our hearts embrace.
Together drawn, in shade and light,
Our art, a masterpiece in sight.

The brush of time, it sweeps away,
Yet echoes linger, here we stay.
In every detail, spirit shines,
A blend of souls, where love entwines.

In every thread, a tale to tell,
Of joy and trials, laughter, spell.
Through designs shared, we paint our fate,
In the design of together, we create.

The Equation of Love

Two hearts collide, a perfect sum,
In moments shared, our spirits hum.
With variables, we start to grow,
The roots run deep, as feelings flow.

With fractions of pain and whole of joy,
Balancing acts, love we employ.
In every solve, we find reprieve,
The equation's true: together, we believe.

Subtract the doubts, add more trust,
In this equation, love is a must.
Multiply the dreams that soar above,
In every answer, the proof is love.

As numbers dance, they twirl and shine,
In the realm of us, all is divine.
The sum of us, a radiant blend,
In the equation of love, there's no end.

The Blueprint of Us

In the quiet corners of our hearts,
We sketch the lines of who we are.
With every color, every part,
A canvas wide, a guiding star.

Together we build, with hands held tight,
Foundations strong, both day and night.
In every laugh, in every tear,
Our story grows, year after year.

Blueprints shift as plans unfold,
In the warmth, our dreams turn bold.
With drafts of hope upon the page,
We find our place as we engage.

Each room adorned with memories bright,
Echoes of love in morning light.
With every stroke, our vision clear,
We create a world, my dear.

So let the pages turn and sway,
In this design, we'll find our way.
Together, we'll shape the fate,
The blueprint of us, oh, how great.

Interlocking Dreams

In fields of color, dreams align,
Two minds entwined, like vine and pine.
With whispered hopes beneath the moon,
We craft a world, a timeless tune.

From distant shores to skies so vast,
Our visions dance, forever cast.
Hand in hand, we chase the light,
In unity, our spirits ignite.

Each dream a thread in fabric spun,
Woven tightly, two become one.
Through stormy nights and sunny days,
Together we walk, in countless ways.

The stars above, a guiding spark,
As we embark through shadows dark.
In every challenge, we are strong,
In interlocking dreams, we belong.

So let us soar, on wings so free,
In this shared vision, just you and me.
With courage, we'll climb every height,
Interlocking dreams, our hearts take flight.

Under the Same Roof

We built a shelter, strong and wide,
With laughter echoing inside.
The walls embrace, with warmth and cheer,
Under the same roof, we draw near.

From morning light to evening dark,
In every corner, love leaves its mark.
Together we dream, together we share,
In the spaces filled with tender care.

Our sanctuary, a safe retreat,
Where every moment feels complete.
With whispered words and loving gaze,
We find our joy in countless ways.

Through stormy weather, through seasons' change,
Our hearts remain steady, never strange.
For every struggle, side by side,
Under the same roof, we abide.

So let the world spin fast and wide,
In this haven, we will reside.
Together we flourish, forever in bloom,
Under the same roof, there's always room.

The Cadence of Commitment

In every heartbeat, a promise made,
A rhythm formed that won't ever fade.
With whispered vows and earnest eyes,
We dance to dreams that never die.

The cadence flows like water's song,
In harmony, where we belong.
Each step we take, a pledge so true,
In this sweet dance, it's me and you.

With laughter leading, we find our pace,
In this commitment, we embrace.
Through ups and downs, we hold the beat,
As life's ballet unfolds, so sweet.

Through trials faced, we stand as one,
In the cadence, our journey's begun.
With every turn, our spirits lift,
In this commitment, life is a gift.

So let the music play on and on,
In the cadence of love, we'll never be gone.
With heartbeats aligned, we'll forever roam,
The cadence of commitment, our eternal home.

The Structure of Together

In dreams, we build our home,
With laughter as our stone.
Each moment, hand in hand,
Together, we shall stand.

Through storms that test our will,
We find the strength to fill.
With love as our command,
Together, we shall stand.

In silence, hearts do speak,
In whispers, futures peek.
Crafting a world so grand,
Together, we shall stand.

With every tear and smile,
We walk a thousand miles.
In every grain of sand,
Together, we shall stand.

In the chapters of our tale,
Together, we prevail.
With hope as our demand,
Together, we shall stand.

Guided by Stars

Beneath the endless night,
We find our way in light.
The constellations sing,
A map of everything.

With every twinkle bright,
Our dreams take flight in sight.
The universe so wide,
In wonder, we abide.

Through cosmic waves, we drift,
In stardust, hearts uplift.
Together, we shall roam,
The heavens call us home.

As galaxies converge,
The universe's urge.
We dance, a silver thread,
In perfect paths we've tread.

When shadows veil our views,
The stars will guide us through.
With every step we take,
Together, we awake.

The Nexus of Love

In every glance we share,
A spark ignites the air.
Through every silent waltz,
We weave no fault, no faults.

In whispers soft and low,
Our hearts begin to grow.
A bridge 'tween you and me,
In love's sweet symphony.

Through tempest, joy, and strife,
We dance the dance of life.
With laughter, tears, and grace,
Together, we find place.

In moments stitched in time,
Each heartbeat is a rhyme.
Connected by a thread,
Where love can ever spread.

As stars align above,
We celebrate our love.
In every beat, we find,
Our souls are intertwined.

The Soundtrack of Us

In melodies so sweet,
Our hearts skip to the beat.
With rhythms, we ignite,
A love in purest light.

In whispers, songs arise,
We dance beneath the skies.
With every note, I feel,
Our love, a grand reveal.

Through laughter, soft refrain,
Our symphony remains.
In harmony, we flow,
Together, let it grow.

As echoes fill the air,
In every breath, a prayer.
The soundtrack of our days,
In wondrous, endless ways.

With every heart's embrace,
We find our perfect place.
In chords that never cease,
Together, live in peace.

Wrenched Gears of Togetherness

In the workshop of dreams we toil,
Wrenched gears turn with love's sweet oil.
A tangle of hands in the shadows bend,
Creating a bond that will never end.

Rusty edges grind away the past,
With each tick forward, shadows cast.
We mend what's broken, piece by piece,
In the heart's embrace, we find our peace.

Together we forge a future bright,
Under the stars, in the cool night light.
Our voices blend like a sweet refrain,
In this grand machine, love's gentle strain.

Each rhythm leads to the next embrace,
In this clock we call our sacred space.
Time may wane and shadows flee,
But in this moment, it's you and me.

So let the gears continue to grind,
Our hearts entwined, forever aligned.
Through trials and joys, we stand as one,
In the wrenched gears, our journey's begun.

The Clockwork of Hearts

Ticking softly, the clockwork sighs,
Each second whispers of truth and lies.
Gears of passion, gentle in their play,
Map the shadows of night and day.

Two hearts wound tight in a shared embrace,
Navigating time at a measured pace.
With every chime, a promise made,
In the dance of time, our fears allayed.

Brass and steel, they come alive,
In rhythms ancient, we learn to thrive.
With each rotation, love gains its might,
Building bridges in the soft moonlight.

Hand in hand through the ticking years,
We navigate laughter, traversing fears.
A clockwork heart beats in sync with mine,
Creating moments, profound and divine.

When the world slows and shadows reign,
Together we'll stand, through sun and rain.
In this clockwork of hearts, we find our fate,
The silence between beats, love resonates.

Companions in Conjunction

In the workshop of our shared delight,
Companions we are, forging through the night.
With hearts aligned, we chase the dawn,
In laughter and dreams, we are reborn.

Two paths converge in a dance so sweet,
Every rhythm uniting, two hearts meet.
Through whispers of love, we intertwine,
Building a journey, yours and mine.

With every challenge, strength we find,
Guided by stars, our spirits combined.
In this sacred place, where the moments fade,
Together we rise, unafraid, unscathed.

So let time's river carve its way,
Side by side, we'll forever stay.
With each step forward, bonds ignite,
Companions in conjunction, hearts take flight.

Together we dream, together we share,
In the tapestry of life, we weave with care.
United in purpose, our spirits soar,
Companions in conjunction, forevermore.

Synchrony of Souls

In the quiet hum of the moonlit night,
Souls synchronize, hearts taking flight.
With every heartbeat, a story unfolds,
In the symphony of love, pure and bold.

Stars align in the canvas above,
Illuminating paths of untold love.
With every whisper, we gently sway,
In this synchrony, we find our way.

Hands entwined, a bond unbreakable,
In the waves of time, undeniably flakable.
Together we navigate the endless sea,
With dreams as our compass, you and me.

In the rhythm of moments, our spirits blend,
With every heartbeat, love's sweet commend.
In this dance of souls, vast and bright,
Together we shine, igniting the night.

So let the world around us spin and twirl,
In this synchrony of souls, we unfurl.
For in every pulse, a universe swells,
In the whispered secrets of love, it dwells.

Ties that Bind

In shadows deep, our whispers weave,
Threads unseen, we dare believe.
Time may twist the paths we roam,
Yet in your heart, I've found a home.

With every laugh, we share a spark,
A bond forged bright, igniting dark.
In silent moments, hands entwined,
Together still, our fates aligned.

Through storms we face, together stand,
With gentle strength, we understand.
Though distance calls, and time moves fast,
Our love remains, forever cast.

In every tear, a story shared,
In whispered dreams, we both have cared.
A legacy of hope we find,
Through every trial, ties that bind.

As seasons shift and ages spin,
Our hearts will dance, where love begins.
In every beat, a timeless rhyme,
Forever yours, through endless time.

The Symphony of Two

In gentle notes, our hearts do play,
A melody that lights the way.
In harmony, we blend and soar,
Together, love, we're evermore.

Each laugh, a chord, a vibrant sound,
In silence, too, our souls are found.
With every touch, a rhythm sweet,
In quiet moments, we're complete.

Through crescendos, highs and lows,
A symphony that ever grows.
In perfect time, our spirits meet,
Two hearts in sync, a dance so fleet.

With every heartbeat, music flows,
In whispered vows, affection shows.
Together we'll compose our tune,
An endless song beneath the moon.

So let us play, through day and night,
In this symphony, pure delight.
For in the blend of me and you,
We find the magic, the love that's true.

Crafting Forever

With gentle hands, we shape our dreams,
Through whispered hopes and sunlight beams.
In every heartbeat, plans unfold,
Crafting forever, a story told.

In every kiss, a promise made,
In storms we face, we won't be swayed.
Together we'll build a lasting art,
Two souls entwined, a growing heart.

With patience strong, our vision clear,
Creating moments we hold dear.
In laughter shared, the years will flow,
An endless journey, love will grow.

Through trials faced and dreams pursued,
In love's embrace, our fortitude.
We craft a life that's deeply ours,
A tapestry of suns and stars.

With every breath, we shape today,
In you I find my path, my way.
Crafting forever, hand in hand,
In this great life, together we stand.

Assembled Souls

In quiet moments, souls align,
A puzzle made, a design divine.
With every laugh, a piece we find,
In this great dance, our hearts entwined.

Through tangled paths, we journey far,
Guided by dreams, like a shining star.
In each embrace, a warmth bestowed,
Together strong, we've built our road.

Through shadows cast, and bright sun's glow,
In every challenge, together grow.
Assembled souls, we rise and shine,
In shared existence, love's true sign.

In whispered words, our spirits merge,
A symphony of love's great surge.
With every heartbeat, we evolve,
In unity, our hearts resolve.

As time goes on and seasons shift,
In love, we've found life's sweetest gift.
Assembled souls, forever new,
Together, my heart belongs to you.

The Collector of Moments

In the quiet of dusk, I stand still,
Gathering whispers of a day's thrill.
Each laugh a jewel, each frown a shard,
Moments like stars, both near and far.

With a breath, I capture the sun's glow,
The warmth of goodbyes, the chill of a blow.
Fragments of life, both fragile and bold,
Tales of the heart that never grow old.

I stitch them together in the fabric of time,
Threads of the mundane, of sorrow, of rhyme.
Each second a treasure, a memory to hold,
In the album of life, where stories are told.

Yet some moments fade like whispers of air,
Captured in silence, too fleeting to share.
But still I collect, with a curious soul,
For the art of remembering makes me feel whole.

As shadows grow long and the night creeps in,
I cradle these moments, both loss and win.
For in this collection, I find my own place,
The Collector of Moments, in time's warm embrace.

A Symphony Unfolding

Notes dance in the air, like petals in spring,
A symphony whispers, ready to sing.
Each sound a heartbeat, a story to tell,
In this grand orchestra, we find our spell.

Strings weave a tale of joy and of tears,
Piano keys echo the laughter and fears.
With every crescendo, emotions arise,
Carried on melodies, like birds in the skies.

The rhythm invites us to sway and to move,
With each passing moment, the world starts to soothe.
In harmony's cradle, we dance and unite,
A tapestry vibrant, painting the night.

Flutes flutter softly, like whispers of morn,
While drums beat the pulse of a love reborn.
Each timbre and tone finds its place in the fold,
A symphony soaring, both tender and bold.

As the final note lingers, fading away,
We bask in the echoes, where memories stay.
For in this grand symphony, we're never apart,
An unfolding of life, a song from the heart.

The Wheel of Together

In the circle of life, we find our way,
Spinning together, come what may.
Each turn a promise, each pause a bond,
In the wheel of together, our spirits respond.

Through storms and sunshine, we lovingly tread,
With hearts intertwined, by hope we are led.
Every laugh shared and every tear cried,
In this wheel of together, we never hide.

As seasons keep changing, we bend and we sway,
Embracing the journey, come night or day.
With courage to face what tomorrow may bring,
The strength of our unity, an unyielding wing.

Through valleys of shadow and peaks kissed by light,
We gather our dreams, and take to flight.
In the rhythm of together, in step we remain,
With love as our compass, through joy and through pain.

So here's to the wheel, steady and true,
Turning with hope and the love that we strew.
For in this great cycle, we find our delight,
The wheel of together, forever in flight.

Uniting Paths

Two roads converge in morning light,
Each step we take feels just so right.
Hand in hand, we walk as one,
Together shining like the sun.

Through the valleys, we will roam,
Finding comfort, we feel at home.
With every turn, our spirits blend,
A journey shared, where love won't end.

In each moment, laughter shared,
A bond so strong, we are prepared.
Facing storms, we stand as two,
Our paths united, strong and true.

In silence, whispers of our dreams,
A tapestry of hopes and schemes.
We dance beneath the stars so bright,
Uniting paths in endless night.

So here we are, with hearts so wide,
Through life's journey, we shall glide.
With every step, our spirits soar,
Together forever, ever more.

The Harmony of Life

In nature's chorus, sweet and clear,
The whispers of the earth we hear.
With every note, the world sings loud,
Embracing all beneath the cloud.

Each season brings its vibrant hue,
From autumn's gold to winter's blue.
In cycles formed, we find our place,
A dance of time, a warm embrace.

The river flows, a melody,
In its soft rush, we feel so free.
With every wave, a tale unfolds,
Of love and loss, of young and old.

In every heartbeat, rhythms play,
Connecting us along the way.
In silence, we hear life's refrain,
A harmony that feels no pain.

So let us join in this sweet song,
Where all belong, where we grow strong.
In unity, our voices rise,
The harmony of life, our prize.

Spinning the Threads

Within the loom, our tales entwine,
Threads of colors, yours with mine.
We weave our stories, strand by strand,
Creating dreams with heart and hand.

Each twist and turn, a choice we make,
In every stitch, a bond we stake.
Through joy and sorrow, our patterns flow,
An intricate dance, a vibrant show.

The fabric of life, both strong and fine,
In every fiber, our hearts align.
With patience fierce and love so deep,
In this tapestry, our secrets keep.

In shadows cast, we find the light,
As we create by day and night.
Together, we craft a unique thread,
In the space where all else is shed.

So let's embrace this artful blend,
The threads of life that never end.
In every piece, a tale unfolds,
The joys of life, the love it holds.

Alloyed Aspirations

In the forge of dreams, we strike with fire,
Molding hopes with deep desire.
With every spark, our visions rise,
Forging futures beneath the skies.

Through trials faced, we learn and grow,
Tempered hearts in the heat of flow.
In alloyed strength, we find our way,
Turning night into gleaming day.

With hands united, we shape the form,
Together, facing every storm.
Each drop of sweat, a testimony,
Of all we've built, of all we see.

In dreams alloyed, we craft a path,
Together facing all the wrath.
With every beat, our spirits soar,
In aspirations that we adore.

So let us rise, like metal bright,
In the furnace of hope, igniting light.
With hearts combined, we stand so tall,
Alloyed aspirations, we will not fall.

Equilibrium of Emotions

In shadows dance the hopes we weave,
A balance found, in hearts we believe.
Joy gently sings, while sorrow sighs,
In this duet, true wisdom lies.

With every heartbeat, a tale unfolds,
A tapestry rich, in threads of gold.
Through laughter's light, through tear's embrace,
We find our way in this sacred space.

The storm may howl, the calm will come,
In chaos, whispers of peace hum.
Together we stand, hand in hand tight,
In harmony's glow, we embrace the night.

The sun will set, the moon will rise,
In twilight's glow, calm us the skies.
For every shadow, a light shall bloom,
In equilibrium, we find our room.

Emotions flow like tides on sand,
Each wave a story, a gentle hand.
Turning our trials into gently spun art,
In the quiet balance, we mend the heart.

The Crafting of Home

In every corner, laughter's sound,
A warmth that wraps, where love is found.
Brick by brick, a story built,
In echoes soft, no trace of guilt.

Windows gleam with morning's light,
A hearth that burns through winter's night.
Walls embrace both joy and sorrow,
In this space, we dream tomorrow.

Each room whispers memories dear,
In every shadow, a tale to clear.
Gathered souls around the table,
In shared stories, love's true label.

Flowers bloom in a garden bright,
Sunshine dances, heart takes flight.
With open doors and hearts in tune,
In the crafting of home, we find our boon.

Foundations strong, yet spirits free,
In our little world, just you and me.
Home is where the heart feels light,
Forever cherished, a pure delight.

Paths United

Two roads diverged, yet we chose one,
In the golden light, our journey begun.
Together we wander, hand in hand,
In unity, we take our stand.

Through valleys deep and mountains high,
With every step, our spirits fly.
In laughter, tears, we stay aligned,
Our souls entwined, our dreams combined.

With every turn, a lesson learned,
In the fire of trust, our hearts have burned.
The road ahead may twist and bend,
But together, our spirits mend.

As seasons change, we walk as one,
In shared sunrises and setting sun.
No matter the storms that come our way,
In paths united, we find our sway.

For every journey leads us near,
To places bright, where love is clear.
In unity, our strength we find,
On this endless path, our hearts entwined.

The Merging of Minds

In quiet corners, thoughts collide,
Like rivers flowing, side by side.
Ideas spark with fierce delight,
In the merging shadows, we ignite.

Each word a brush on canvas bare,
Creating worlds with love and care.
In dialogue rich, we seek the core,
Unlocking doors, we thirst for more.

From different skies, our visions sing,
In harmony, our spirits bring.
With every question, walls will fall,
In the dance of reason, we stand tall.

Thoughts intertwine like roots in ground,
In diverse soil, new dreams are found.
Through every challenge, we rise anew,
In the merging of minds, our hopes accrue.

In conversations deep, we find our place,
A symphony of thoughts, a warm embrace.
Together we ponder, together we climb,
In the art of sharing, we beat time.

Pulley of Promises

In whispers soft, the dreams arise,
With every pull, the future flies.
A tapestry of hopes we weave,
In trust, we learn, in faith, believe.

The weight of words can shift the skies,
Each promise made, a new sunrise.
Together strong, we lift our gaze,
In every heart, a spark ablaze.

Through trials faced, our spirits grow,
A chain unbroken, love will flow.
With every inch, we rise anew,
Bound by the dreams that guide us true.

In silence shared, we find our way,
Each moment lived, a bright display.
Connected here, our hopes will meet,
In unity, our lives complete.

With every shift, we stand as one,
The pulley spins, our journey begun.
Linked in purpose, hand in hand,
Across the skies, our promises stand.

The Foundation of Fellowship

In the quiet night, friendships form,
With every laugh, our hearts are warm.
Through trials faced and joys we share,
A bond unbroken, always there.

Together we rise, hand in hand,
A tapestry of love, so grand.
In every moment, trust is laid,
The foundation strong, never to fade.

With open hearts, we share our dreams,
In every challenge, or so it seems.
Together we stand, never alone,
In this embrace, we find our home.

Through storms we weather, side by side,
In fellowship, we take our stride.
Each story shared, a bridge we build,
With every bond, our hearts fulfilled.

In laughter's echo, in silence too,
The strength we find in me and you.
Rooted deep, our spirits soar,
In unity, we seek for more.

A Circuit of Kindred Spirits

In the electric hum of shared delight,
Kindred spirits dance in the night.
With every spark, we come alive,
A circuit strong, where dreams contrive.

Through laughter loud and whispers sweet,
We find our rhythm, hearts in beat.
In shared stories, our spirits blend,
Each voice a note that will not end.

Connected souls, we light the way,
In every moment, come what may.
Through storms we clutch, our courage bold,
In this circuit, our lives unfold.

Like stars aligned, we shine so bright,
Illuminating the darkest night.
In vibrant colors, dreams appear,
With kindred spirits, we persevere.

Together we rise, in this embrace,
A lasting bond, a sacred space.
In harmony, our hearts ignite,
In this circuit, pure delight.

Forging Futures Together

In the furnace of our shared desire,
We mold the dreams, with vision dire.
With every strike, we shape our fate,
In unity, we'll orchestrate.

Hands intertwined, we break the mold,
In every heartbeat, a story told.
Through trials faced, our metals blend,
Forging futures, hand in hand, my friend.

With passion fierce and courage high,
We build our hopes, we touch the sky.
In every challenge, strength we find,
The path ahead, forever kind.

In the heat of dreams, we learn to grow,
With every failure, a brighter glow.
Together bound, we face the storm,
In forging futures, love transforms.

With hearts aflame, we take the lead,
In shared ambition, we plant the seed.
Together we rise, forever true,
In this journey, me and you.

Tension and Release

In quiet moments where silence reigns,
The weight of the world in subtle chains.
Breath held tight, heartbeat's dance,
Within the shadows, secret romance.

A gentle sigh, the pressure unfolds,
Fear dissipates, as courage holds.
With every pulse, the strain takes flight,
In the embrace of the soft moonlight.

Battles fought within the chest,
Yearning soul seeking rest.
With every kiss of the summer breeze,
Tension melts, life finds ease.

In the push and pull of night and day,
We learn to find our own sweet way.
A song of hope, a whispered prayer,
In tension's grip, love's threads we share.

Through the chaos, where hearts intertwine,
Release is born when spirits align.
An open heart, a guiding hand,
In the depth of trust, together we stand.

The Gearbox of Commitment

Rusty cogs and shifting gears,
Love's mechanics through the years.
Each promise spun, a sturdy thread,
In the dance of life, our path is led.

Turning wheels, the laughter's sound,
In every turn, our hopes are found.
Oil of trust, it keeps us sane,
In the gearbox, all joy and pain.

Moments shared in precision's grace,
In the rush of life, we find our pace.
With every challenge, each bend and twist,
Commitment's bloom, we can't resist.

Like clockwork hearts, we beat in time,
Building our story, line by line.
Hand in hand through thick and thin,
In the gearbox, our love begins.

A mechanic's heart, tender and true,
Each wrench and bolt, a bond we grew.
In every journey, every mile,
The gearbox spins, the world a smile.

Interlocking Rings

Two circles traced in endless gold,
Binding stories yet untold.
A promise sealed in silent night,
Interlocking rings, our future bright.

Each twist and turn, a journey shared,
In the dance of life, we've boldly dared.
The world outside may be unknown,
In this bond, we have grown.

Through storms and sun, our hands meet tight,
Woven together in pure delight.
Symbols of faith, the ties we wear,
Interlocking rings, a love laid bare.

In moments quiet, hearts collide,
A dance of trust we cannot hide.
Through trials faced and joy embraced,
With every glance, our love is graced.

These golden loops, unbroken, round,
In each heartbeat, our dreams rebound.
Together we stand, forever strong,
In interlocking rings, we belong.

Choreography of Connection

In the rhythm of life, we learn to sway,
Steps intertwined, come what may.
A dance of souls in perfect sync,
In the flow of time, we find our link.

Turns and twists, our hearts take flight,
In the embrace of the soft twilight.
With every leap, we dare to dream,
Choreography of love, a flowing stream.

The music plays, and we take our chance,
Spinning together in a timeless dance.
With every touch, we feel the spark,
In this cosmic waltz, we leave our mark.

Through laughter shared and tears we shed,
In every moment, love is spread.
The stage is set, the lights aglow,
In this connection, we learn and grow.

As we move through the seasons of life,
With grace and poise, amid the strife.
In the quiet whispers and joyful song,
The choreography of connection is where we belong.

Synergy of Souls

In the quiet chambers where souls entwine,
Whispers of warmth in the soft moonshine.
Fear dissolves in the glow of trust,
Hearts align, harmonizing, as they must.

In laughter shared, and in tears released,
Time stands still; in joy, we're pleased.
Threads of kindness weave through our days,
In this embrace, love forever stays.

Voices echo in a sacred tone,
Two minds unite, no longer alone.
Moments blend like colors in art,
Each stroke a testament, a beating heart.

Through storms we dance, through calm we sail,
Together we flourish; together we fail.
In unity, fierce, we rise and fall,
Synergy sparkles, binding us all.

With gentle strength, we push and pull,
A perfect balance, a mutual lull.
In every glance, a story told,
The magic of synergy, a treasure of gold.

Building Blocks of Togetherness

Each moment cherished, lets memories grow,
Like bricks laid down, a foundation we know.
Together we build, with laughter and dreams,
A fortress of love, stronger than it seems.

With every challenge, we gather and rise,
Layer by layer, reaching for the skies.
Hand in hand, we shape our fate,
Crafting a path together, never too late.

The mortar of kindness, the sand of grace,
In the warmth of home, we find our place.
Connected through heartbeats, both fast and slow,
In this bustling life, our roots entwine and flow.

We carve our names on the walls of time,
With love as the cornerstone, silent yet sublime.
Each heartbeat echoes in voices that cheer,
Building togetherness, year after year.

Like rivers converging, our paths combine,
Creating a landscape, a love so divine.
In unity's strength, our spirits enhance,
With every heartbeat, we dance our dance.

The Continuum of Connection

In every glance, a spark ignites,
A bridge across seemingly endless nights.
Threads of fate weave 'round our souls,
A continuum of connection, as time unfolds.

Through valleys deep and mountains high,
Our hearts converse, with no need for why.
In the silence, a rhythm so clear,
The pulse of togetherness draws us near.

Like seasons changing, we ebb and flow,
In the garden of trust, love continues to grow.
Each moment a step on this winding road,
In connection we travel, lightening the load.

With every breath, we share the air,
In the tapestry of life, we stitch with care.
A bond unbroken, through laughter and tears,
The continuum of connection conquers our fears.

So let us wander through this divine maze,
Hand in hand, in love's gentle praise.
For in this journey, we'll always find,
The threads of connection, beautifully intertwined.

Nesting Hearts

In a cozy corner, our hearts reside,
In woven dreams and the love we bide.
Soft whispers linger in shadows' embrace,
Nesting together, we find our place.

With gentle warmth, we craft our nest,
Filling it with moments that feel the best.
Together we flutter, like birds in flight,
In this sacred space, everything feels right.

Through storms that rage, and winds that howl,
Our hearts entwined, we learn to prowl.
Cocooned in love, where we safely rest,
In the arms of each other, we are blessed.

With every sunrise, our hopes arise,
Painting the dawn in our shared skies.
Two souls united, our journey starts,
Creating a haven, in nesting hearts.

So here we'll stay, in joy and fear,
In the rhythm of laughter, we'll persevere.
For in this love, our spirits soar,
Nesting together, forevermore.

The Compass of Companionship

In every storm, you guide my way,
A beacon bright that won't decay.
Through laughter's light and sorrow's night,
Together we stand, always in sight.

With every step, our bond grows strong,
In silence sweet, where hearts belong.
Navigating life, side by side,
In this journey, you'll be my guide.

Through valleys deep and mountains high,
Your laughter rings, a heartfelt sigh.
In moments shared, love's compass turns,
A path to warmth, where passion burns.

No distance vast can pull apart,
Two souls entwined, a beating heart.
For every trial, we find our way,
With you, my friend, come what may.

In twilight's glow, our dreams align,
In whispers soft, your hand in mine.
The journey's long, but love's the map,
Together we'll dream, on this path we tap.

Wires of Wedded Joy

In gentle loops, our lives entwine,
Connected sparks that brightly shine.
Through every trial, laughter flows,
In wedded bliss, our union grows.

With every glance, a tender touch,
In rhythms shared, we feel so much.
In morning light and evening's call,
Our love withstands, it conquers all.

With whispered dreams and bonds so tight,
In the dark we find our light.
Through tangled paths, we weave our fate,
In every heartbeat, we celebrate.

The wires run deep, electric and grand,
United we stand, hand in hand.
In playful sights and joyous tears,
We build a life that perseveres.

Each day a gift, each moment dear,
With you, my love, I have no fear.
In harmony, we craft our song,
Through life together, where we belong.

Seams of Shared Dreams

In every stitch, our hopes are sewn,
A tapestry of dreams we've grown.
With every thread, a vision bright,
In whispers soft, we chase the light.

Through laughter shared, we weave our days,
In moments cherished, love conveys.
In twilight's hue, our visions meld,
In silence found, our hearts are held.

With patterns formed and colors bold,
Our dreams unite, a tale retold.
In seams that bind, we find our way,
Together we share each passing day.

As sometimes frayed, our cloth may show,
In mending, love continues to grow.
With every patch, a memory dear,
We stitch our path, through joy and fear.

In dreams of old and those yet seen,
We craft a life, a journey keen.
Together through time, we will prevail,
In seams of dreams our hearts set sail.

The Anvil of Affection

Upon this anvil, hearts do meet,
Where love is forged, a bond so sweet.
With gentle taps, we shape our fate,
In fiery warmth, we cultivate.

Through trials hard, our strength is shown,
In every blow, affection grown.
With every spark, our spirits fly,
Together we reach for the open sky.

In cooling moments, love remains,
In tempered steel, our joy sustains.
With every curve, our journey bends,
In the anvil's grace, our lives transcends.

In quiet hours, we mold the dreams,
With every heartbeat, love redeems.
Through laughter bright and shadows deep,
On this anvil, our promises keep.

So let us craft our days with care,
In every moment, our souls laid bare.
In this embrace, we find our way,
On the anvil of love, come what may.

Strings Attached: A Duet.

In the quiet of the night,
Two voices softly blend,
Whispers dance in the air,
Melodies never end.

Fingers trace the shadows,
Where the heartbeats align,
With every note, a promise,
In perfect time, we shine.

Through the laughter and sorrow,
Our song will always soar,
When the world fades to silence,
Together, we'll encore.

Bound by the threads of music,
No distance can divide,
In this duet we flourish,
Side by side, our pride.

Every chord a reminder,
Of love that's tried and true,
In the symphony of life,
It's always me and you.

The Gears of Togetherness

In the clock of our moments,
Gears mesh and turn with ease,
Ticking to a rhythm,
We move just like the breeze.

With every twist and motion,
Time dances in our hands,
Crafting memories together,
Like grains of golden sands.

When the storms begin to stir,
And shadows loom ahead,
We find strength in our bond,
In love, we're always led.

The whispers of our secrets,
Like cogs, keep turning fine,
In the heart of the twilight,
Our spirits intertwine.

So let the clock keep ticking,
We'll navigate each hour,
In the gears of togetherness,
Our love will always tower.

Clockwork Hearts

In the center of our story,
Two hearts beat in a line,
Like gears in perfect motion,
Together, we define.

Underneath the softest glow,
Time bends to our embrace,
As seconds turn to hours,
In love, we find our place.

Every tick a shared heartbeat,
Every tock a gentle sigh,
We dance upon the moments,
As time begins to fly.

With hands that twist in unity,
And voices soft and low,
Clockwork hearts are timeless,
In sync, we always flow.

When the world calls on us,
And chaos reigns the day,
We simply find our rhythm,
And let the music play.

Harmonized Connections

In the tapestry of life,
We weave our threads in gold,
Each stitch a shared connection,
A story to be told.

From the mountains to the valleys,
Our paths forever blend,
In every note we sing,
Each heart, a faithful friend.

When silence fills the air,
With worry's heavy tone,
We find strength in our chorus,
We're never lost, alone.

The chords of understanding,
Create an endless tune,
In the night, we harmonize,
Beneath the silver moon.

With every breath we gather,
New colors in our art,
Harmonized connections,
Two souls, one beating heart.

Under One Canopy

Beneath the broad and leafy tree,
We find a world where we can be.
The whispers of the gentle breeze,
Speak softly of our shared unease.

In dappled light, we weave our dreams,
Through sunlit paths and moonlit beams.
With every step, our shadows blend,
A sacred bond that won't transcend.

The roots run deep, entwined below,
A testament to love's sweet glow.
Together we will face the storms,
With arms entwined, our hearts are warm.

Through changing seasons, rain or shine,
We share our joys, our hearts align.
In quiet moments, laughter rings,
United here beneath our wings.

So let the stars above us shine,
Their light a guide, our spirits twine.
Under one canopy, we stand,
Two souls entwined, hand in hand.

The Threading of Hearts

In silence, threads begin to weave,
A tapestry that does not leave.
Each stitch a promise, strong and true,
A path designed for me and you.

Through colors bright and shadows cast,
We stitch the future from the past.
Each golden line, a tale to tell,
In intricate patterns, we both dwell.

With every heartbeat, ties grow tight,
Binding us through day and night.
Connections formed with gentle care,
Interlaced love is always there.

The fabric shifts with every sigh,
Yet through it all, we learn to fly.
With threads of hope, we are renewed,
In every moment, grace imbued.

Together woven, side by side,
In this great journey, we confide.
The threading of our hearts remains,
A work of art that love sustains.

Synchronizing Souls

In quiet spaces, voices blend,
A melody where hearts transcend.
With every note, our spirits rise,
In harmony beneath the skies.

We move as one, our steps align,
Like stars that twinkle, brightly shine.
The rhythm of our breaths, a song,
Together facing what feels wrong.

Each moment stacked, like layers deep,
In subtle beats, our secrets keep.
A dance we learn, in trust we flow,
Synchronizing love as we grow.

Through every change, we twist and turn,
With every lesson, love we learn.
United paths that gently curl,
In this fine dance, we both unfurl.

So let us sway, beneath the moon,
In this embrace, we find our tune.
Synchronizing souls, a perfect match,
In every moment, love we catch.

The Choreography of Us

In a world where shadows twine,
We find a stage that's solely mine.
With every glance, a silent cue,
The choreography of me and you.

We spin in circles, hearts allowed,
With graceful moves that feel so proud.
Each leap a testament to trust,
In steps where only love is just.

Through whispered rhythms, we engage,
Writing chapters page by page.
The dance unfolds, a soul's delight,
In every moment, pure and bright.

With every turn, we feel the spark,
A tango painted in the dark.
Our bodies sway, like branches flow,
The choreography is love's gentle glow.

In this embrace, we find our place,
With every heartbeat, we interlace.
Together here, we celebrate,
The dance of us—a perfect fate.

The Art of Together

In every laugh, a shared delight,
In every tear, a bond made tight.
We weave our stories, side by side,
In the warmth of hearts, love cannot hide.

Fingers entwined, we dance through days,
With whispered dreams, in tender ways.
The art of together, a canvas bright,
Painted with colors of purest light.

Through storms we sail, through trials we grow,
In each other's eyes, our true selves show.
A masterpiece formed, every stroke divine,
In this dance of life, forever entwined.

The silence speaks, when words can't form,
In the stillness, we find our norm.
Together we rise, we laugh and we fall,
The art of together, it conquers all.

In shades of dusk, as the sun fades low,
Still, our hearts in harmony glow.
With every heartbeat, our love a song,
In the art of together, we forever belong.

Layers of Affection

Beneath the smiles, there lie deep hues,
Layers of affection, old and new.
Each glance a story, each touch a thread,
Woven with care, in words unsaid.

The first layers fragile, tender and light,
Like budding flowers in morning's bright.
As seasons change, we build and grow,
Through every layer, our love will show.

In quiet moments, the layers reveal,
The warmth of connection that both can feel.
A touch, a laugh, a gentle embrace,
Layers of affection, time can't erase.

With every challenge, we uncover more,
Stronger each time, at the very core.
Layer upon layer, a fortress we build,
In the depth of our love, our hearts are filled.

Under the surface, the roots intertwine,
The layers of affection, forever align.
Through storms and sunshine, through joy and strife,
Each layer a testament to the beauty of life.

Intertwined Fates

In the quiet moments, fate takes its hold,
Intertwined paths, a story unfolds.
Two souls connected, in ways unforeseen,
Bound by the threads of a silken dream.

From distant places, we drift and we roam,
Finding in each other, a place called home.
With every heartbeat, the cosmos aligns,
Intertwined fates in the stars, it shines.

Through laughter and tears, a tapestry we weave,
In the fabric of life, we learn to believe.
Each twist and turn, a dance on the road,
Intertwined fates, together we're bold.

The winds may change, but still we remain,
Through every trial, through joy and pain.
Our fates like ribbons, forever entwined,
In this journey of hearts, true love we find.

As we walk forward, hand in hand,
Intertwined fates, in a world so grand.
With every sunset, our spirits soar,
Together forever, forevermore.

The Uncharted Path

In the wilderness of thoughts, we tread,
The uncharted path, where few have led.
With every step, uncertainty looms,
Yet in your presence, my spirit blooms.

Through tangled vines and shades of green,
We explore the whispers of what could be.
Together we search for what lies ahead,
In the heart of the forest, where dreams are fed.

The compass of hope, it guides our way,
In the uncharted path, we choose to stay.
With courage as our shield, we venture forth,
In the dance of discovery, we find our worth.

The horizon calls with a radiant glow,
In the uncharted path, together we grow.
Through sun and shadow, we'll bravely roam,
In each other's arms, we've found a home.

As stars emerge in the evening sky,
With dreams as our map, together we fly.
The journey is endless, the stories we weave,
On the uncharted path, a life to believe.

Harmonizing Hopes

In whispers soft, our dreams arise,
A symphony beneath the skies.
Each note a wish, each chord a prayer,
Together, we shall find our air.

With hearts aligned, we lift our voice,
In unity, we make our choice.
To chase the light, to brave the storm,
In this embrace, we feel the warm.

The echoes dance on gentle wings,
In harmony, the future sings.
With every step, with every glance,
We weave our fate, we take our chance.

Through shadows deep, through valleys low,
Our hopes will guide the way we go.
In vibrant hues, in tones so bright,
Together, we ignite the night.

So let the stars our path define,
With dreams that spark like vintage wine.
In laughter shared, in love expressed,
We find our home, we find our rest.

The Assembly of Us

In circles round, we gather here,
With laughter bright and voices clear.
Each story shared, each hand we hold,
In kindness wrapped, our hearts unfold.

The strength we find in unity,
A tapestry of you and me.
With every glance and every cheer,
We build a space where all is dear.

Through trials faced, through joy combined,
In every moment, peace we find.
With open hearts, we pave the way,
In all our colors, bold and gay.

We lift each soul, we raise each dream,
With gentle words, we find the theme.
An assembly of diverse delight,
Together we are strength and light.

So let us stand, let voices rise,
In harmony beneath the skies.
For in this bond, we truly see,
A world of love and unity.

Lattice of Lives

In woven threads, our lives entwine,
A lattice formed, a design divine.
Through joy and pain, we interlace,
In every stitch, a sacred place.

With whispers soft, we share our fears,
In colors bright, we paint our tears.
Each laugh a spark, each cry a thread,
In tapestry, our stories spread.

Through seasons change, through time's embrace,
We find our strength in every space.
With hands that reach, with hearts that blend,
A lattice strong that will not bend.

In shadows cast, in sunlight's glow,
Our spirits rise and ebb like flow.
Interwoven dreams, we dare to chase,
In the tapestry, we find our grace.

So let us weave, let's join our parts,
In this grand work of tender arts.
Through every layer, rich and vast,
Our lattice holds the future cast.

The Tools of Tenderness

With gentle hands, we shape our days,
In tender ways, our love displays.
Each smile a tool, each kind remark,
We build a flame from tiny spark.

In empathy, we carve the space,
Where hearts can rest and find their grace.
With patient hearts, we mend the breaks,
In every bond, true love awakes.

Through whispered thoughts, through caring deeds,
We plant the love that ever feeds.
With every hug, with every touch,
We craft a world that means so much.

The tools we wield, so soft yet strong,
In every note, we find our song.
With each embrace, a shelter made,
In tender acts, our fears allayed.

So let us share, let kindness reign,
With tools of love, we break the chain.
For in our hands, we hold the flame,
Of tenderness that knows no name.